"Every child is
an artist; the
problem is how
to remain an
artist once he
grows up."

PABLO PICASSO

The life of a man is a circle from childhood to childhood, and so it is in everything where power moves. Even the seasons form a great circle in their changing, and always come back again to where they were. The sun comes forth and goes down again in a circle. The moon does the same, and both are round. Birds make their nests in circles, for theirs is the same religion as ours. The wind, in its greatest power, whirls. The sky is round, and I have heard that the earth is round like a ball, and so are all the stars. Everything the Power of the World does is done in a circle.

6699

BLACK ELK

relaxation
COLOR *yourself* CALM

Mandalas by
Paul Heussenstamm

BARRON'S

Introduction

Relaxation

Blue-Green Mandala

Dark Beauty

Chartre Moon

Eye on Wisdom

Gold Star

Golden Flower

Healing Hands

Healing Presence

Inner Worlds

Maok Kingdom

Kaleidoscope

Mayan Dream

Lotus Mandala

Nine Keys

North Star

Inner Dimension

Palimino's Leap

Petals of the Soul

Paradise Valley

Eye of Contemplation

Purple Flames

Tiki Man

Swimming with the Mermaids

Red Pearl

Spiraling Flower Road

New Blossoming of the Soul

The White Owl's Dream

Umbrella Tree

Time Before Morning

Sleeping Beauty

About the quotes

About the illustrator

INTRODUCTION

Welcome to the world of mandalas and the beginning of your journey to becoming more focused and centered by coloring your mind calm. This mindfulness-inspired coloring book includes 30 original color mandalas with their accompanying black-and-white templates to color in, which will expand your self-awareness and open the door into your own creativity.

Mandalas are an ancient form of meditative art. Simply put, the mandala is a design that draws your eye toward its center, which focuses your mind on the present moment and opens up your heart.

Within our fast-paced society, we are often in our minds rather than in our hearts—our minds then become closed to creativity, relaxation, or happiness. Once you begin to color in the mandalas, your center will begin to shift from your mind and into your heart. The core of the mandala then becomes the center of your heart. Importantly, once your heart is open your creativity naturally pours forth.

Coloring in mandalas relaxes the mind, body, and spirit; relieves stress; and is a chance to explore your own inner creativity. For the past 25 years, I have been exploring, painting, practicing, and teaching the art of mandala painting. The first thing you should know is that coloring mandalas requires no previous experience or innate artistic talent. As a teacher, the hardest task is to dispel the worries of students and banish any thoughts that they are not creative and are not naturally artistic.

The key to mandala coloring is to simply take the time to sit quietly, to focus your mind, and to begin coloring. This is precisely how I started my journey of coloring and painting mandalas way back in the late 1980s. At first, I did it for fun, but it then led to a profound change in my lifestyle. It makes no difference if you color in a single mandala or one thousand mandalas, it is merely the practice of centering yourself through creativity and relaxation, which ultimately leads to increased happiness.

Art is transformative. Mandala coloring transforms your attitude toward life and develops your consciousness. When you reach this meditative state through coloring, your body becomes more sensitive, your eyes see more deeply, and you will feel more intensely.

Congratulations on arriving at this point. You will now discover that as you begin to color in these mandalas your awareness will expand. As your awareness expands, and the more you color, you will begin to look and feel more deeply into the mandalas. Essentially, as you open up to see inside the mandala you are simultaneously opening up yourself.

A mandala is a very ancient guide that symbolically allows you to look into yourself. The process of coloring in a mandala can give you profound insights into your psyche and your mind. It appears simple, yet there are layers of growth, understanding, and even a transforming of consciousness that are revealed in a mandala painting, whether coloring one in or simply looking at one. The key to mandala meditation is to sit still and gaze at one. Once you have colored in several mandalas—or even several parts of one mandala—you will begin to feel and see patterns within yourself. This is deeply valuable because it allows you to recognize your own inner patterns and it helps you to communicate with your conscious self through the core patterns.

RELAXATION

ACCEPTANCE

Participation in creative pursuits shifts your center from your mind to your heart, which increases your happiness. I have been teaching creative courses for the past 25 years and I always tell my students that when you take one of my workshops you must step outside of your conscious mind and open up your channels of creativity.

EXISTENCE

When you engage with this inner creativity, your otherwise narrow world is transformed into an infinite universe. When I am immersed in any creative process, I exist outside of time and space, but I equally feel incredibly connected to the universe as a whole.

CONNECTIVITY

On the deepest level, the artist is a conduit—the mandalas are paintings that are simply a passage for their creator. The beauty of creative pursuits is that once your heart is open and you are fully connected to the infinite universe, creativity naturally spills forth. Someone who has never considered himself/herself a creative can, in an instant, experience a shift in his/her existence.

TRANSFORMATION

Creativity can radically alter your perspective. The wonderful thing about coloring mandalas is that once you learn the practice, coloring is easily shareable with friends, with loved ones, and with children.

STILLNESS

When coloring mandalas, you can no longer think about blues, purples, or greens in the same way. Thoughts become colors. Colors become patterns. Patterns awaken the soul. Coloring becomes magic. From deep within, you will feel stillness and relaxation, because the colors shine through you. Your mind shifts from the logical and reasoning left brain to the intuitive and emotional right brain.

ATTAINMENT

As you begin to access your inner creativity, while also allowing yourself the time, patience, and focus to color yourself calm, your perspectives and outlook on life will change. Transformation is a form of happiness that wells up from your core being. This attainment of joy will most likely be beyond anything you have ever felt before.

TRANSMITTANCE

In becoming an artist, you are making something that you love, while also touching others on a very deep level. After you have colored in each of your chosen mandalas, take a photograph or scan your creation and share it on social media with the hashtag #coloryourselfcalm so that people all over the world can enjoy your creativity. This creates a form of shared happiness that no words can do justice.

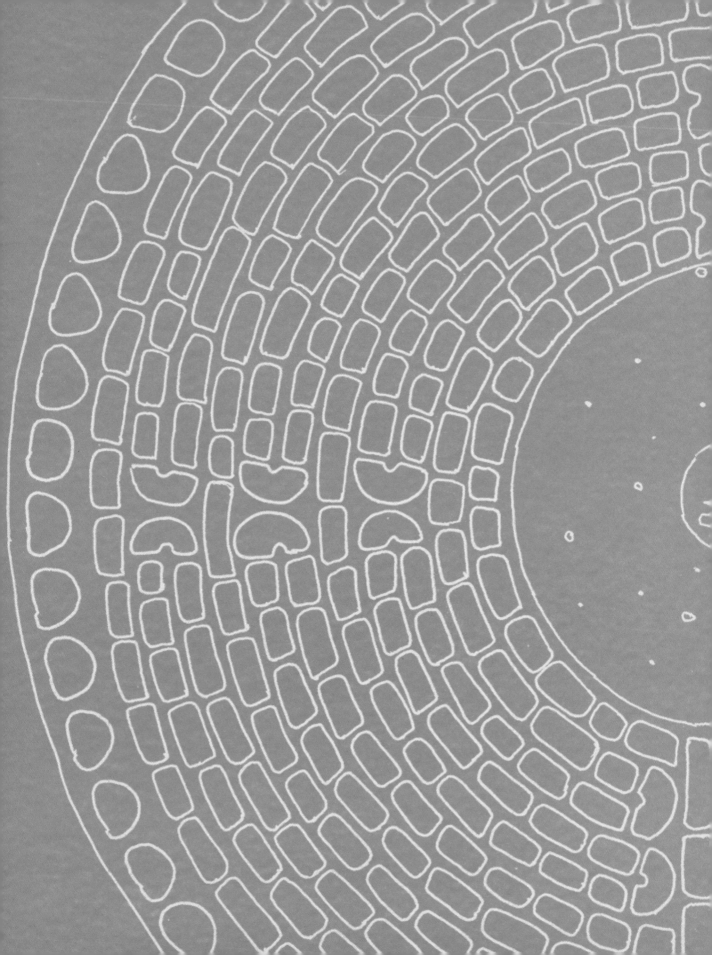

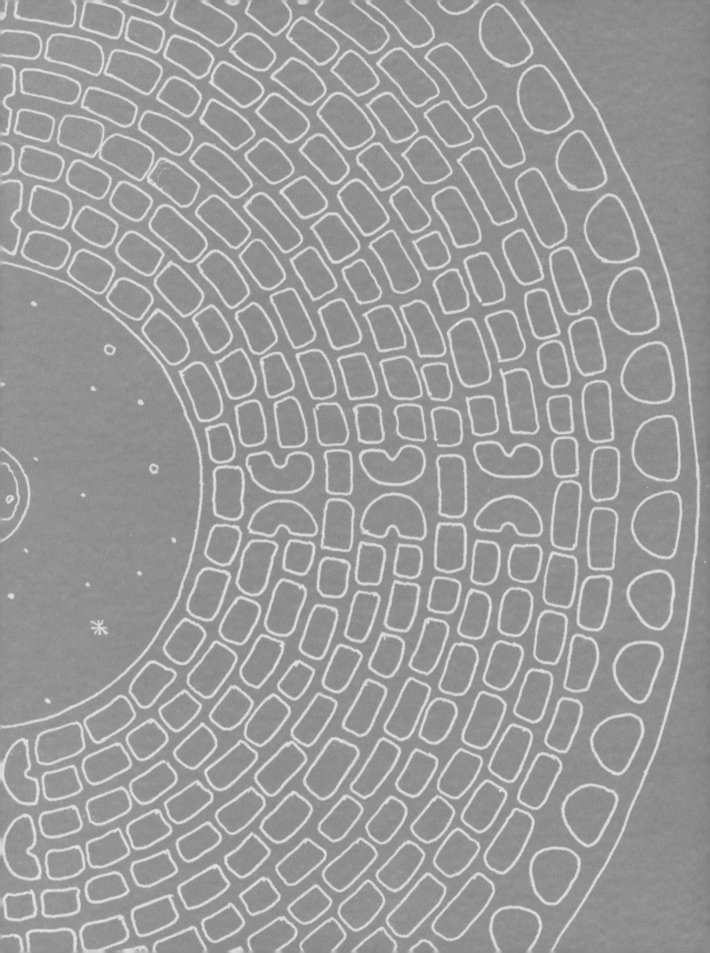

Blue-Green Mandala

When you are creating a mandala, you go to places that you
cannot access anywhere else in life. Places that are usually hidden
become accessible to the mandala painter.

Dark Beauty

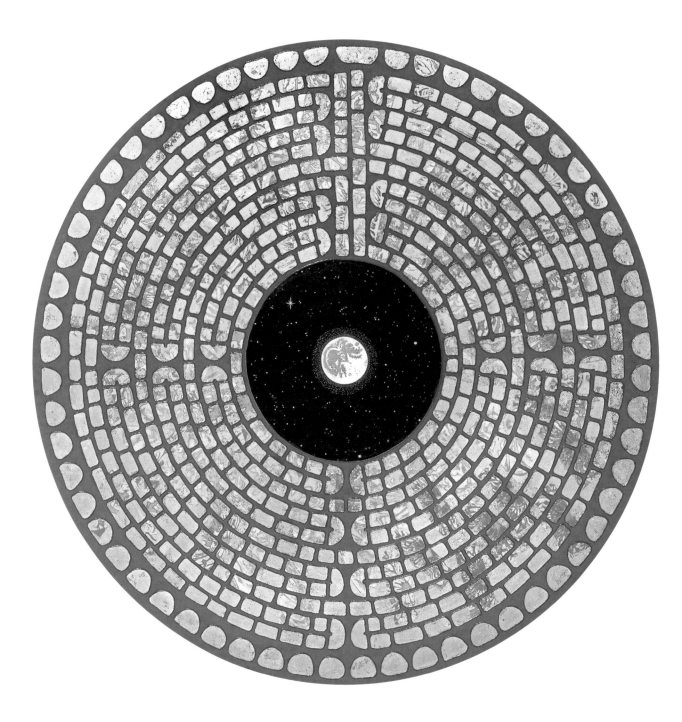

Chartre Moon

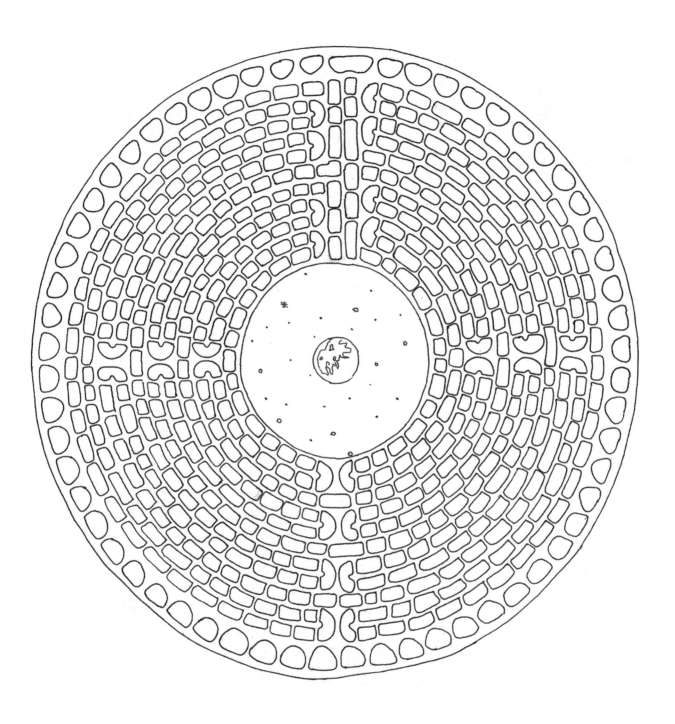

"It's not a matter of painting life, it's a matter of giving life to painting."
PIERRE BONNARD

Eye on Wisdom

Gold Star

"In art you have to learn to see and feel something that is beyond the ordinary vision and feeling, to go within and bring out from there deeper things."
MOTHER MEERA

Golden Flower

Healing Hands

An artist speaks the universe's messages.

Healing Presence

Inner Worlds

When a mandala's image comes to me, I go into the realm of art and it's
all downloaded there, every detail.

Maok Kingdom

Kaleidoscope

"Painting is with me but another word for feeling."
JOHN CONSTABLE

Mayan Dream

Lotus Mandala

A mandala painting is a ball of light in the artist's hand.

Nine Keys

North Star

"Most modern painters work from a different source, they work from within."
JACKSON POLLOCK

Inner Dimension

Palimino's Leap

"The role of the artist is to ask questions, not answer them."
ANTON CHEKHOV

Petals of the Soul

Paradise Valley

"When you create there is an added energy that surpasses anything else."
LOUISE NEVELSON

Eye of Contemplation

Purple Flames

When you are painting a mandala, you start off as an individual and then begin to realize that you are deeply connected to all the other painters in a non-dual universe.

Tiki Man

Swimming with the Mermaids

"Art evokes the mystery without which the world would not exist."
RENÉ MAGRITTE

Red Pearl

Spiraling Flower Road

When you create, you start to experience a different way of living.

New Blossoming of the Soul

The White Owl's Dream

"The life that is not examined is not worth living."
PLATO

Umbrella Tree

Time Before Morning

Once you experience the beauty of the mandala,
it is hard to deny your own inner beauty.

Sleeping Beauty

QUOTES ARE TAKEN FROM:

PABLO PICASSO was one of the greatest and most influential artists of the twentieth century, as well as the cocreator and leading exponent of Cubism.

BLACK ELK was a famous holy man, traditional healer, and visionary of the North American tribe of Oglala Lakota (Sioux).

PIERRE BONNARD was an early twentieth-century French painter who, as part of the Symbolist movement, painted scenes of simple, domestic daily life.

MOTHER MEERA is an Indian avatar, believed by her devotees to be an embodiment of the Divine Mother or Shakti.

JOHN CONSTABLE was a famous landscape painter in eighteenth-century England, who sketched in the open-air and then worked up these sketches into large exhibition paintings.

JACKSON POLLOCK was a famous twentieth-century artist who revolutionized the world of modern art with his abstract expressionist painting techniques, which involved pouring paint directly onto the canvas.

ANTON CHEKHOV was a Russian physician and author.

LOUISE NEVELSON was a Russian-born sculptor known for her monochromatic abstract expressionist works that challenged the notions of stereotypical male sculptural style.

RENÉ MAGRITTE was a Belgian Surrealist artist, renowned for his witty and thought-provoking paintings that gave new meanings to everyday objects.

PLATO was one of the most important Greek philosophers. He founded the Academy in Athens and was a student of Socrates and taught Aristotle.

PAUL HEUSSENSTAMM

Paul Heussenstamm is a master painter of mandalas and other forms of spiritual paintings. He has painted and drawn over 1,000 mandalas and has taught worldwide for 25 years, as well as at his studio in California.

Since 1996, he has worked for the Chopra Center for Wellbeing, sharing his art at almost every major event that Deepak Chopra hosts. He is the sanctuary artist at the Agape International Spiritual Center in Culver City in California, which has 10,000 local members.

Publishing director Sarah Lavelle
Commissioning editor Lisa Pendreigh
Creative director Helen Lewis
Designer Emily Lapworth
Production director Vincent Smith
Production controller Stephen Lang

First edition for North America published in 2016
by Barron's Educational Series, Inc.

First published in 2015 by
Quadrille Publishing
www.quadrille.co.uk

Quadrille is an imprint of Hardie Grant.
www.hardiegrant.com.au

All inquiries should be addressed to:
Barron's Educational Series, Inc.
250 Wireless Boulevard
Hauppauge, NY 11788
www.barronseduc.com

ISBN: 978-1-4380-0839-4

Printed in China

9 8 7 6 5 4 3 2

For best results, colored pencils are recommended.